W9-AQW-141

50 STATES TO CELEBRATE

Celebrating
ILLINOIS

Text copyright © 2014 by Marion Dane Bauer
Cover and interior illustrations copyright © 2014 by C. B. Canga
Country and state map illustrations copyright © 2014 by Jennifer Thermes

All rights reserved. Green Light Readers and its logo are trademarks of Houghton Mifflin
Harcourt Publishing Company, registered in the United States of America and/or its jurisdictions.

For information about permission to reproduce selections from this book,
write to Permissions, Houghton Mifflin Harcourt Publishing Company,
215 Park Avenue South, New York, New York 10003.

www.hmhbooks.com

The text of this book is set in Weidemann.
The display type is set in Bernard Gothic.
The illustrations are drawn with pencil and colored digitally.
The maps are pen, ink, and watercolor.

Photograph of white-tailed deer buck on page 32 © 2014 by Photodisc/Getty Images
Photograph of cardinal perched on a tree branch on page 32 © 2014 by ©gregg williams/Fotolia
Photograph of blue violet on page 32 © 2014 by Royal Freedman/Alamy

Library of Congress Cataloging-in-Publication Data
Bauer, Marion Dane.
Celebrating Illinois / Marion Dane Bauer.
p. cm. — (Green light readers level 3) (50 states to celebrate)
ISBN 978-0-544-12375-5 paperback
ISBN 978-0-544-12900-9 paper over board
1. Illinois—Juvenile literature. I. Title.
F541.3.B38 2014
977.3—dc23
2013006334

Manufactured in China
SCP 10 9 8 7 6 5 4 3 2 1
4500454442

50 STATES TO CELEBRATE

Celebrating
ILLINOIS

Written by **Marion Dane Bauer**
Illustrated by **C. B. Canga**

ESSAMINE COUNTY PUBLIC LIBRARY
600 South Main Street
Nicholasville, KY 40356

Houghton Mifflin Harcourt
Boston   New York

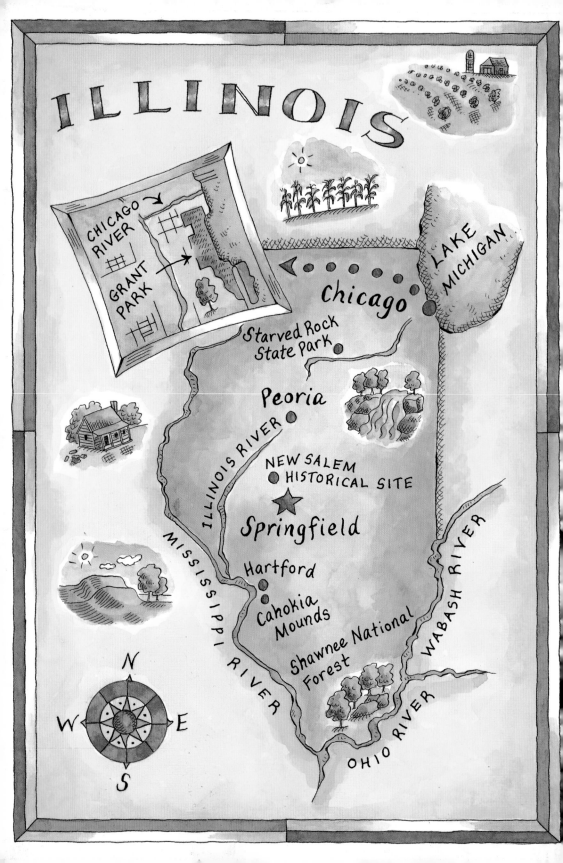

Hi! I'm Mr. Geo.

Today, I am visiting the **Prairie** State.

It's also called the Land of Lincoln.

That's right! I'm in Illinois.

Can you find Illinois on a map?
It's near the middle of the country.
Look south of Wisconsin.

2

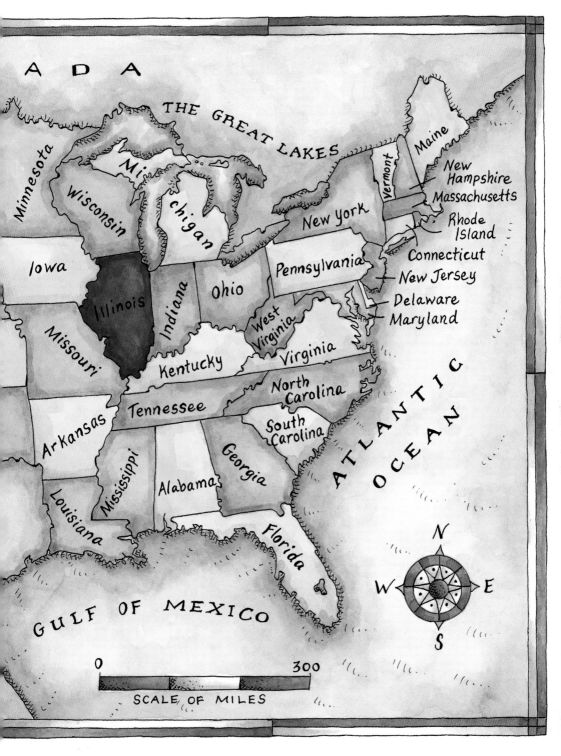

Look west of Indiana.
Now look east of Iowa and Missouri.
That state with a lot of squiggly borders is Illinois!

Let's start in the Windy City of Chicago.
Here I am at a kids' kite festival.
Expert kite flyers demonstrate their skills for us.

I got to design and fly my own kite!
Does it remind you of someone?

Chicago is located on the shore of Lake Michigan.
Grant Park lies between the lake and downtown.

Lake Michigan is one of five Great Lakes.
The other ones are Lake Erie, Lake Huron,
Lake Superior, and Lake Ontario.

My favorite spot in the park? Buckingham Fountain.
The fountain puts on a water show
every 20 minutes.
When it's lit up at night, it's dazzling!
So is the skyline!

Chicago is the home of the very first **skyscraper**.
It had 10 floors and rose 138 feet high.
It was built after the **Great Chicago Fire**
destroyed much of the city in 1871.

A stone water tower was one of the few
structures to survive the Great Chicago Fire.
It is still standing.

Today, Chicago's tallest building is Willis Tower.

It soars 1,450 feet.

It has 110 floors!

But it's hard to see them all from way down here!

The elevated train—called the "L"—is a great way to explore Chicago.
We can loop around downtown or travel to the neighborhoods.

I love discovering new restaurants
and specialty grocers.
So many foods from so many different **cultures!**
What do I crave most when I'm here?
A Chicago-style hot dog with all the toppings.
Mustard, relish, pickles, onions, peppers, and
tomatoes, please!

The deep-dish pizza was invented in
Chicago in 1943.

Chicago has many museums.
Here I am at the Field Museum of
Natural History.
Did you ever see such a big creature?
Sue is the world's largest and most complete
Tyrannosaurus rex skeleton.

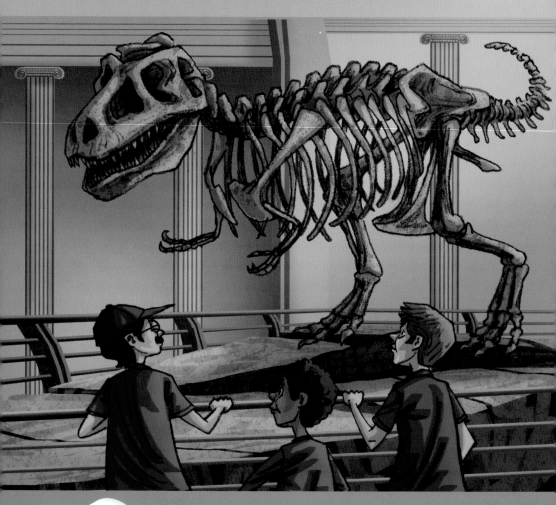

At the Museum of Science and Industry,
you can watch 12 moving robots assemble
and package toy tops.

Navy Pier offers all kinds of entertainment.
I sailed on a tall ship.
I saw musical fireworks!
But the most fun of all?
The swinging carousel!
Whee!

Chicago is a big sports town.

It even has two baseball teams.

Shhhh! Don't tell anyone . . .

I'm going to cheer for the Chicago Cubs today . . .

and root for the Chicago White Sox tomorrow!

WRIGLEY FIELD

HOME OF

CHICAGO CUBS

WELCOME

I'm not big enough to play for the Chicago Bears.
I'm not tall enough to play for the Chicago Bulls.
But maybe I'm fast enough to skate
with the Chicago Blackhawks!

Chicago's soccer team is called
Chicago Fire.

Illinois was once mostly prairie and forest.

Now it is full of farmland.

Corn and soybean fields spread for miles and miles.

This tractor gives me a great view *and* a bumpy ride!

The southern part of the state has high ridges and
deep valleys.
I love hiking in the **Garden of the Gods**
in Shawnee National Forest.
Look! That rock formation is shaped a little like
a camel.

Illinois is far from any ocean, yet it is near
lots of water.
To the north is Lake Michigan.
To the east, there are the Wabash and Ohio Rivers.
In the middle, there is the Illinois River.
And the Mississippi River marks
the entire western border.
These waterways are often used to transport goods.

But they make great playgrounds, too!

In 1848 a new **canal** connected Lake Michigan to the Illinois and Mississippi Rivers. It let ships travel from the Great Lakes to the Gulf of Mexico.

Long ago, Native Americans known as
Mound Builders lived in what is now Illinois.
Between 1050 and 1150 these people built a
great city.

The Cahokia Mounds are what is left of that city.

Monks Mound is one of the largest.

I climbed all 100 feet to the top!

Did you know?

Many Illinois towns and cities have Native American names—Algonquin, Peoria, Skokie, and Oswego are just a few.

The French were the first Europeans to see Illinois.
Louis Jolliet, an explorer, and Jacques Marquette,
a priest, arrived by canoe from **Quebec** in 1673.
They traveled south on small streams and big rivers.

All around, the land was **fertile** and full of wildlife.

Fur traders and settlers came next.

The French named this place Illinois after

the **Illiniwek** people, who lived here already.

In 1804, explorers Meriwether Lewis and William Clark prepared for their **expedition** west at Camp River Dubois, near Hartford, Illinois.

Illinois has many heroes, but few are more admired than Abraham Lincoln, our 16th president. The New Salem State Historic Site recreates the village where Lincoln lived as a young man. I like sampling **frontier** life!

Lincoln was a lawyer in Springfield, the state capital.
We can visit his home and his law office here.
And we can pay our respects at Lincoln's **tomb**.

President Abraham Lincoln helped bring
an end to slavery in our country.

Illinois is known for dramatic weather.
Sometimes it's really, really cold.

And sometimes it's very, very hot.

Other times, cool air blowing across the
flat land from the north meets warm air
coming from the south.
Thunderstorms, tornadoes, and blizzards
are often the result.
Most people here like having four seasons, though.
As for me, I'm glad I packed my raincoat!

Here I am at Starved Rock State Park.

It is a place of great beauty.

Waterfalls and **canyons** are everywhere.

Fish are plentiful too.

But I plan to come again in January, when
thousands of bald eagles flock here.
I hear it is a remarkable sight to see!

29

Illinois is near the center of our large country.
This location makes it a hub for
transportation and travel.
Our nation's second busiest airport is here.
Trains and trucks crisscross through, day and night.

Ships and barges make their way from port to port.
It is a gateway east, west, north, and south!
I'm not sure I'm ready to say goodbye, though.
There is so much more to discover in Illinois!

Fast Facts About Illinois

Nickname: The Prairie State, also the Land of Lincoln.

State motto: State Sovereignty, National Union.

State capital: Springfield.

Other major cities: Aurora, Chicago, Joliet, Naperville, Rockford.

Year of statehood: 1818.

State animal: White-tailed deer.

State bird: Northern cardinal.

State flower: Native violet.

State flag:

Population: More than 12.8 million according to the 2010 census.

Fun fact: Chicago is called the Windy City not because a lot of wind blows through, but because some folks thought that people from Chicago were a bit "windy," meaning they liked to boast about Chicago.

Dates in Illinois History

1050: An estimated 20,000 Native Americans live in Cahokia.

1673: Louis Jolliet, a French-Canadian explorer, and Jacques Marquette, a Jesuit priest, explore Illinois by canoe. They travel down the Mississippi River into what is now Arkansas.

1763: Great Britain gains control of the area, now known as Illinois, from France.

1783: The treaty ending the **American Revolution** gives the United States control of the land west of the original 13 colonies, including Illinois.

1818: Illinois becomes the 21st state.

1848: The Illinois and Michigan Canal is completed.

1861: Abraham Lincoln becomes president of the United States.

1871: Fire destroys much of Chicago.

1973: The Sears Tower is completed, becoming for a time the world's tallest building. The building is now called Willis Tower.

1998: With Michael Jordan's help, the Chicago Bulls win their sixth NBA championship.

2000: Sue, the largest, most complete, and best-preserved *Tyrannosaurus rex* ever found, is put on display in Chicago's Field Museum.

2006: Millenium Park in Chicago gains a new attraction nicknamed "The Bean," a huge bean-shaped sculpture with a shiny, silvery surface that reflects the skyline.

2009: Barack Obama, a senator from Illinois, becomes the first African American president of the United States.

Activities

1. **LOCATE** the five states that border Illinois using the map on pages 2 and 3. **SAY** each state's name out loud and whether it is located north, south, east, or west of Illinois.

2. **CREATE** a small brochure about Illinois by folding a sheet of paper in half. Then **DRAW** pictures in each section of the paper (front and back) about exciting things to see or do in Illinois. Underneath each picture, write a sentence that tells people about the things you chose draw.

3. **SHARE** two facts you learned about Illinois with a family member or friend.

4. **PRETEND** you traveled to Illinois with Mr. Geo. Your classmates have lots of questions about the state. Answer the following questions for them correctly and you will be named Student of the Week.

    a. **WHO** were the first people of European descent to explore what is now Illinois?

    b. **WHAT** are two important farm products grown in Illinois?

    c. **WHERE** is the Field Museum of Natural History?

    d. **WHEN** did the Great Chicago Fire happen?

    e. **WHICH** president lived in Illinois when it was still frontier land?

5. **UNJUMBLE** these words that have something to do with Illinois. Write your answers on a separate sheet of paper.

    a. **ARIRPIE** (**HINT:** a place with tall grass)

    b. **CRESPRKSAYS** (**HINT:** Chicago has many of these tall buildings)

    c. **YBSNOEA** (**HINT:** a crop)

    d. **CLILNON** (**HINT:** a president)

    e. **GEALE** (**HINT:** a bird)

Glossary

American Revolution: the war that won the 13 American colonies freedom from British rule; it took place from 1775–83. (p. 33)

canal: a waterway that is dug to connect bodies of water so ships can move between them. (p. 19)

canyon: a deep valley with steep, rocky walls on both sides. A canyon is formed when rivers or streams wash away soil and rock over a long period of time. (p. 28)

cultures: the customs, beliefs, and ways of living shared by a group of people. (p. 11)

expedition: a journey made for a definite purpose. One of the main purposes of the Louis and Clark Expedition was to find the most direct route from the Midwest to the Pacific Ocean through uncharted western territory. The expedition was commissioned by President Thomas Jefferson and took place from 1804–6. (p. 23)

fertile: good for plants to grow in. (p. 23)

frontier: region that is just beyond or at the edge of a newly settled area. (p. 24)

Garden of the Gods: an area of stunning rock formations in Shawnee Forest National Park in Illinois. (p. 17)

Great Chicago Fire: a massive fire that burned much of downtown Chicago in 1871. The fire started in a barn around 9:00 p.m. on October 8 and lasted 27 hours. (p. 8)

Illiniwek: Native American people from about 12 different tribes who lived in Illinois and other midwestern states. These tribes included the Cahokia, Kaskakia, and Peoria, among many others. (p. 23)

prairie: a wide area of flat or rolling land with tall grass and few trees. (p. 1)